Guide to Webpack

Practical Guide

A. De Quattro

Copyright © 2024

Practical Guide

1.Introduction to Webpack

Webpack is a *module bundler* for modern web applications, allowing you to combine various assets like JavaScript files, CSS, images, and HTML into a single optimized package. Created to address the complexities of managing modules and dependencies within web applications, Webpack has become the de facto standard for frontend development. With its ability to handle resources efficiently, Webpack reduces page load times and improves the overall performance of web applications. This section will explore the fundamental concepts of Webpack, explaining what makes it such a powerful and versatile tool in web development.

1.2 History and Evolution of Webpack

Webpack was first introduced in 2012, at a time when frontend development was becoming increasingly complex. Initially created by Tobias Koppers, Webpack was designed to solve issues related to dependency management in JavaScript projects. Before its inception, developers used tools like Grunt and Gulp, which focused primarily on task running rather than module management. Webpack revolutionized how developers manage their assets by introducing the concept of the module. Over the years, Webpack has seen exponential growth in terms of popularity and functionality, becoming one of the most widely used tools in web development. This section will review the history and evolution of Webpack, highlighting key released versions and introduced innovations.

1.2.1 The Origins of Webpack

This subsection will delve into the historical context and needs that led to the creation of Webpack. It will cover the period before its introduction, when developers relied on tools like RequireJS or Browserify for module management. The limitations of these tools, particularly in terms of scalability and flexibility, will be discussed, as well as how Webpack addressed these issues by introducing a more robust and efficient *module bundling* system.

1.2.2 The Early Versions of Webpack

Here, the focus will be on the early versions of Webpack, particularly version 1, and how it began changing the way developers managed dependencies and modules in their projects. The initial community adoption, early challenges, and the first innovations that made Webpack a compelling alternative to existing tools will be described.

1.2.3 The Evolution with Webpack 2 and 3

This section will cover the evolution of Webpack with versions 2 and 3. With

Webpack 2, fundamental features like native ES6 Module support, *tree shaking* for dead code elimination, and a more flexible and powerful configuration system were introduced. Webpack 3 saw further performance optimizations and an improved development experience. Improvements in modularity and customization, which made Webpack even more adaptable to projects of varying complexity, will also be discussed.

1.2.4 The Revolution of Webpack 4 and 5

This subsection will examine Webpack versions 4 and 5, which marked a significant turning point in the tool's evolution. With Webpack 4, the concept of "zero configuration" became a reality, allowing developers to start using Webpack without the need for complex configuration files. Notable improvements in speed and optimization, such as *split chunks* and the *side effects flag*, were also introduced. Webpack 5, the latest major version, brought further innovations, such as support for module federation, even more efficient dependency management, and better compatibility with the modern development ecosystem. This part will also delve into the challenges faced during the transition between versions and the impact these innovations had on the developer community.

1.3 Use Cases for Webpack

This section will explore the various scenarios where Webpack can be used to improve asset and dependency management within a project. Although commonly associated with JavaScript project management, Webpack is an incredibly flexible tool that can be adapted to a wide range of development needs. Practical use cases will be discussed, ranging from building complex web applications to managing simple static sites, highlighting how Webpack can simplify and optimize the development process.

1.3.1 Single-Page Applications (SPA)

This subsection will delve into how Webpack is particularly useful for managing single-page applications (SPAs). SPAs, which load a single HTML page and dynamically update content without reloading the entire page, require an efficient system for managing modules and dependencies. Webpack provides tools like bundle size optimization, *code splitting*, and asynchronous module loading, which are essential to ensure that the application remains fast and responsive. Examples of how Webpack can be configured to efficiently handle loading and updating components in an SPA will be provided.

1.3.2 Multilingual and Localization Projects

This subsection will discuss the use of Webpack in multilingual and localized projects. Managing multilingual resources, such as translation files and localized content, can be complex, but Webpack simplifies this process through dynamic imports and locale-specific bundles. This allows for loading only the resources needed for a specific language or region, reducing initial load and improving the user experience.

1.3.3 Managing Static Assets

Webpack is also a powerful tool for managing static assets like images, fonts, and CSS files. This section will explore how to configure Webpack to handle these files efficiently, including using specific loaders such as `file-loader`, `url-loader`, and `css-loader`. Methods for optimizing images, managing SVG files as React components, and including fonts in the bundle to ensure optimal performance and visual quality will be discussed.

1.3.4 Performance Optimization

This chapter will address performance optimization through Webpack. Beyond simple *bundling*, Webpack offers a range of tools to enhance application performance, such as file minification, *tree shaking* to remove unused code, and *lazy loading* to load only the necessary resources. Examples of advanced configurations to achieve optimal performance, especially in large projects, will be provided.

1.3.5 Integration with Other Build Tools

Webpack is highly flexible and can be integrated with other build and automation tools like Gulp, Grunt, and npm scripts. This section will explore how to use Webpack in combination with these tools to create customized and powerful workflows. Examples of combining Webpack with task runners and automation tools for tasks like linting, testing, and deployment will be presented.

1.3.6 Server-Side Rendering (SSR) Projects

This section will discuss using Webpack for projects that require server-side rendering (SSR). SSR is a technique that generates the HTML of the application on the server, improving initial load time and SEO optimization. Webpack can be configured to handle both client-side and server-side bundles, allowing developers to use the same code for both server and client rendering. Examples of integrating Webpack into SSR projects using frameworks like Next.js and Nuxt.js will be discussed.

1.3.7 Dependency and External Module Management

This part will explore how Webpack manages dependencies and external modules. As modern applications become more complex, properly managing dependencies becomes essential to avoid conflicts and ensure code cohesion. Webpack offers various strategies for including external libraries, such as using *externals* and managing CommonJS and AMD modules. Configuring Webpack to load specific libraries only when needed, thereby reducing the overall bundle size, will also be discussed.

1.3.8 Build Process Automation

Automating the build process is crucial for improving productivity and ensuring code quality. This section will explore how to configure Webpack to automate different stages of the build process, such as linting, minification, and testing. Examples of automation scripts integrated with Continuous Integration (CI) tools like Jenkins or GitLab CI will be presented to make the build process more robust and efficient.

1.3.9 Modular and Microfrontend Applications

Modular applications and microfrontends represent a growing trend in web application development. Webpack provides advanced tools for managing modular architecture, allowing you to split a complex application into independent parts that can be developed and deployed separately. This section will explore how to configure Webpack to support microfrontends, enabling independent modules to be loaded at runtime and reducing the overall complexity of the codebase.

1.3.10 Library and Framework Development

Webpack is not only a tool for web application development but is also extremely useful for developing libraries and frameworks. This section will cover how to configure Webpack to create modular and reusable packages for distribution via npm or other package managers. Topics such as output configuration, peer dependency management, and creating optimized bundles for different environments, both Node.js and browser, will be discussed.

2. Installing and Configuring Webpack

This section of the manual will provide a detailed guide on how to install and configure Webpack in a project. Starting from the basics of installation, it will then move on to advanced configuration, exploring the various available options and how to customize Webpack to suit the specific needs of your project.

2.1 Prerequisites

This subsection will list the prerequisites for installing Webpack, such as the need to have Node.js and npm installed on your system. Detailed instructions on how to install these dependencies on various platforms (Windows, macOS, Linux) will be provided.

2.2 Installing Webpack

Here, different methods of installing Webpack will be described, both globally and locally within a project. Instructions for installation via npm will be provided, and the differences between global and local installations will be discussed.

2.3 Basic Configuration

This section will explore the basic configuration of Webpack. It will explain how to create a `webpack.config.js` file, describing fundamental options such as `entry`, `output`, and `mode`. Examples of basic configurations sufficient to start working with Webpack in a simple project will be provided.

2.4 Advanced Configuration

This part of the manual will cover advanced Webpack configurations. Options such as configuring loaders, plugins, and optimizations will be explored. Examples of complex configurations for real-world projects, explaining how to leverage Webpack's full potential, will be provided.

3. Core Concepts of Webpack

This section will delve into the core concepts that form the foundation of Webpack, explaining how each part contributes to the module bundling process. Understanding these core concepts is crucial for effectively using Webpack in your projects.

3.1 Modules and Bundles

This subsection will explain the concepts of modules and bundles in Webpack. It will cover how Webpack treats different types of files (JavaScript, CSS, images) as modules and combines them into bundles.

Understanding this fundamental concept is key to grasping how Webpack manages and optimizes assets.

3.2 Loaders

Loaders are essential components in Webpack that transform files into modules. This part will describe the purpose of loaders and provide examples of commonly used loaders, such as `babel-loader`, `css-loader`, and `file-loader`. Instructions on how to configure loaders and integrate them into the build process will be given.

3.3 Plugins

Plugins extend Webpack's functionality and can be used to perform a wide range of tasks, such as optimizing bundles, generating HTML files, and managing environment variables. This section will introduce the concept of plugins, provide examples of popular plugins, and explain how to configure and use them effectively.

3.4 Entry and Output

The `entry` and `output` options in the Webpack configuration file define the starting point of the application and how the bundles should be output. This part will explore how to configure these options, providing examples of different scenarios and explaining how to control the output of the build process.

3.5 Development Server

Webpack's development server (`webpack-dev-server`) provides features like live reloading and hot module replacement, which are essential for a smooth development experience. This subsection will explain how to configure and use the development server, including examples of different configuration options.

4. Working with Loaders

Loaders are a critical component of Webpack that allow you to process various file types and transform them into modules. This section will explore how to use and configure loaders to handle different types of assets within your project.

4.1 JavaScript Loaders

This subsection will cover JavaScript loaders, including `babel-loader`, which enables the use of modern JavaScript features by transpiling code to a compatible version for older browsers. Examples of configuring and using `babel-loader` will be provided.

4.2 CSS and Style Loaders

Managing CSS and other style files is crucial for modern web development. This part will explore loaders like `css-loader`, `style-loader`, and `postcss-loader`, explaining how they process and bundle CSS files. Examples of configurations for handling CSS, Sass, and Less will be provided.

4.3 File and Asset Loaders

Handling static assets like images, fonts, and other files requires specific loaders. This section will describe loaders such as `file-loader`, `url-loader`, and `asset/resource`, explaining how they work and how to configure them for different types of assets.

4.4 Handling Non-JavaScript Assets

In addition to JavaScript, Webpack can manage various other types of files, such as HTML and JSON. This part will explain how to use loaders to process these files, providing examples of configurations for handling

HTML templates and JSON data.

5. Working with Plugins

Plugins extend Webpack's functionality and can be used to perform a variety of tasks beyond simple module bundling. This section will explore how to use and configure plugins to enhance your Webpack build process.

5.1 Optimization Plugins

Optimization plugins are used to improve the performance and efficiency of the build process. This subsection will cover plugins such as `TerserPlugin` for JavaScript minification, `MiniCssExtractPlugin` for extracting CSS into separate files, and others that help optimize bundle size and load times.

5.2 HTML and Template Plugins

Plugins like `HtmlWebpackPlugin` and `WebpackManifestPlugin` help manage HTML files and templates. This section will explain how these plugins work and how to configure them to automatically generate HTML files and manage assets in your project.

5.3 Development Plugins

Development plugins enhance the development experience by providing features like hot module replacement and live reloading. This part will explore plugins such as `HotModuleReplacementPlugin` and `WebpackDevServer` for improving the development workflow.

5.4 Environment Plugins

Managing environment variables and configurations is crucial for building applications that work across different environments (development, production, staging). This section will explain how to use plugins like `DefinePlugin` and `EnvironmentPlugin` to manage environment-specific settings.

6. Performance Optimization

Optimizing the performance of your Webpack build process and resulting application is essential for providing a fast and smooth user experience. This section will cover various techniques and strategies for improving performance.

6.1 Code Splitting

Code splitting allows you to divide your application into smaller bundles, which can be loaded on demand. This subsection will explain the different strategies for code splitting, including dynamic imports and the `SplitChunksPlugin`, and how to configure them effectively.

6.2 Tree Shaking

Tree shaking is a technique for removing unused code from your bundles, reducing their size and improving load times. This part will explore how tree shaking works in Webpack, including configuration options and best practices for ensuring that unused code is eliminated.

6.3 Caching and Hashing

Caching and hashing are important for ensuring that browsers efficiently cache your assets and update them only when necessary. This section will explain how to configure caching and hashing in Webpack to improve performance and ensure that users receive the latest versions of your files.

6.4 Minimization and Compression

Minimizing and compressing your assets can significantly reduce their size, leading to faster load times. This subsection will cover techniques for minifying JavaScript and CSS, as well as using plugins for compression, such as `CompressionPlugin` and `GzipPlugin`.

6.5 Analyzing Bundle Size

Analyzing the size of your bundles can help identify areas for optimization and improvement. This part will explore tools and techniques for analyzing bundle size, such as `webpack-bundle-analyzer`, and how to use the insights gained to optimize your build process.

7. Common Issues and Troubleshooting

This section will address common issues and problems that developers may encounter when using Webpack. Practical tips and troubleshooting steps will be provided to help resolve issues and ensure a smooth development experience.

7.1 Debugging Webpack Configurations

Debugging Webpack configurations can be challenging. This subsection will provide tips and techniques for identifying and fixing issues in your `webpack.config.js` file, including how to use Webpack's built-in debugging features.

7.2 Resolving Loader and Plugin Errors

Loader and plugin errors are common issues in Webpack development. This part will cover how to troubleshoot and resolve errors related to loaders and plugins, including checking configurations, resolving dependency conflicts, and understanding error messages.

7.3 Performance Bottlenecks

Identifying and addressing performance bottlenecks is crucial for optimizing your build process. This section will provide strategies for detecting and resolving performance issues, including analyzing build times, optimizing configurations, and using performance profiling tools.

7.4 Compatibility Issues

Compatibility issues with different versions of Webpack, loaders, and plugins can arise. This subsection will discuss how to handle compatibility problems, including updating dependencies, using version-specific configurations, and leveraging community resources for support.

8. Advanced Topics

For those who want to delve deeper into Webpack's capabilities, this section will cover advanced topics and techniques for optimizing and customizing your Webpack setup.

8.1 Custom Webpack Plugins

Creating custom Webpack plugins allows you to extend Webpack's functionality to suit specific needs. This subsection will provide an overview of how to develop your own plugins, including examples and best practices for writing effective plugins.

8.2 Webpack in CI/CD Pipelines

Integrating Webpack into Continuous Integration and Continuous Deployment (CI/CD) pipelines is essential for automated builds and deployments. This part will explore how to configure Webpack for CI/CD environments, including setting up build scripts, running tests, and automating deployments.

8.3 Advanced Performance Optimization

Advanced performance optimization techniques go beyond the basics. This section will cover more sophisticated methods for optimizing build times and runtime performance, such as advanced code splitting strategies, optimizing asset delivery, and leveraging Webpack's internal APIs for custom optimizations.

8.4 Migrating Between Webpack Versions

Migrating between different versions of Webpack can be complex, especially when major changes are introduced. This subsection will provide guidance on how to handle version migrations, including updating configurations, addressing deprecated features, and leveraging migration tools and resources.

8.5 Integrating Webpack with Other Tools

Webpack can be integrated with a variety of other tools and technologies to enhance your development workflow. This section will explore how to use Webpack in combination with tools like Babel, ESLint, and testing frameworks to create a powerful and efficient development environment.

9. Best Practices

Following best practices ensures that your Webpack configuration is efficient, maintainable, and scalable. This section will outline best practices for using Webpack effectively, including configuration tips, performance optimization, and code organization strategies.

9.1 Structuring Webpack Configurations

Properly structuring your Webpack configuration files is crucial for maintainability and readability. This subsection will provide guidelines for organizing configurations, using multiple configuration files, and managing complex setups.

9.2 Managing Dependencies

Managing dependencies effectively helps prevent conflicts and ensures a smooth development process. This part will cover best practices for handling dependencies, including updating packages, managing version compatibility, and using tools like `npm` and `yarn`.

9.3 Writing Maintainable Code

Writing maintainable code is essential for long-term project success. This section will provide tips for writing clean, modular, and maintainable code in Webpack configurations, including using comments, organizing code logically, and following coding standards.

9.4 Ensuring Consistent Builds

Ensuring consistent builds across different environments is crucial for avoiding issues and maintaining quality. This subsection will cover best practices for achieving consistent builds, including using environment variables, standardizing configurations, and testing build processes.

9.5 Security Considerations

Security is an important aspect of web development. This part will explore security best practices for Webpack, including handling sensitive information, protecting against vulnerabilities, and ensuring that your build process does not introduce security risks.

This structure provides a comprehensive overview of Webpack and its components, offering detailed explanations, practical examples, and best practices for effectively using Webpack in web development projects.

2. Webpack Installation and Configuration

1. System Requirements

Before proceeding with the installation of Webpack, it's important to ensure that your system meets the necessary requirements to properly run the development environment. Since Webpack is a tool based on Node.js, it requires Node.js and npm (Node Package Manager) to be installed on your system.

1.1 Node.js and npm

Node.js is an open-source platform that allows you to execute JavaScript code outside of a browser, providing a fast and scalable runtime environment. npm is the default package manager for Node.js and allows you to install, manage, and distribute software packages written in JavaScript.

1.1.1 Installing Node.js and npm

To install Node.js and npm, you can follow the steps below:

- **Windows**:

  1. Download the Node.js installer from the official website nodejs.org.

  2. Run the installer and follow the instructions. The Node.js installer includes npm by default.

- **macOS**:

  1. You can install Node.js using the Homebrew package manager. If Homebrew is not installed, you can install it by following the instructions on brew.sh.

  2. Once Homebrew is installed, run the following command:

     ```bash
     ```

brew install node
```

This will install both Node.js and npm.

- **Linux**:

1. On Debian/Ubuntu-based distributions, you can use the following command:

```bash
sudo apt-get update
sudo apt-get install nodejs npm
```

2. On Red Hat/CentOS-based distributions, use the command:

```bash
sudo yum install nodejs npm
```

1.1.2 Verifying the Installation
```

After installing Node.js and npm, you can verify that the installation was successful by running the following commands in the terminal:

```bash
node -v
npm -v
```

These commands should return the installed versions of Node.js and npm, confirming that they are correctly installed.

1.2 Other Requirements

Although Node.js and npm are the only mandatory software requirements, some projects may require additional tools for source code management, such as Git, or specific environments for frontend development, like an advanced text editor (e.g., Visual Studio Code, Sublime Text, or Atom).

2. Installing Webpack via npm

Once Node.js and npm are installed, you are ready to install Webpack in your project. There are two main ways to install Webpack: globally or locally.

2.1 Local Installation of Webpack

Local installation is the most common and recommended practice, as it ensures that Webpack is installed as a project dependency and can be used by all team members working on the same project, regardless of the version of Webpack installed globally on their systems.

To install Webpack locally, navigate to your

project directory via the terminal and run the following commands:

```bash
npm install --save-dev webpack webpack-cli
```

This command will install Webpack and Webpack CLI as development dependencies (`--save-dev`) and create a `node_modules` folder within your project, where all installed packages will be placed.

2.2 Global Installation of Webpack

Global installation of Webpack allows you to use the `webpack` command directly from the terminal, regardless of the project you're working on. However, it's important to note that this method may cause conflicts between different versions of Webpack in different projects.

To install Webpack globally, run the following command:

```bash
npm install -g webpack webpack-cli
```

After the global installation, you can verify that Webpack has been installed correctly by running the command:

```bash
webpack -v
```

This command should return the installed version of Webpack.

3. Creating Your First Webpack Project

Now that Webpack is installed, you can start configuring your first project. Follow these steps to create a simple project using Webpack.

3.1 Creating the Project Structure

Start by creating a new folder for your project and navigate inside it:

```bash
mkdir my-webpack-project
cd my-webpack-project
```

Inside the project folder, create the following folders and files:

```bash
mkdir src
```

```
touch src/index.js

touch index.html
```

- `src/index.js`: This is the main JavaScript file that Webpack will use as the entry point.

- `index.html`: A simple HTML file to display the output of your project.

3.2 Configuring the Project with npm

Initialize the project with npm by running:

```bash
npm init -y
```

This command will create a `package.json`

file with default settings, which will contain all the project's dependencies and scripts.

3.3 Configuring Webpack

Now you can configure Webpack to process the JavaScript file and generate a bundle. Start by creating a `webpack.config.js` configuration file in the project's root directory:

```bash
touch webpack.config.js
```

4. Structure of a Configuration File (webpack.config.js)

The `webpack.config.js` file is where you define how Webpack should process your project's files. Below is a basic configuration:

```javascript
const path = require('path');

module.exports = {
  entry: './src/index.js',
  output: {
    filename: 'bundle.js',
    path: path.resolve(__dirname, 'dist')
  },
  mode: 'development'
};
```

4.1 Entry

The `entry` option specifies the entry file that Webpack will use to start building the dependency graph. In this case, `entry:

`'./src/index.js'` tells Webpack to start from the `src/index.js` file.

4.2 Output

The `output` option defines where Webpack should save the generated bundle. `filename: 'bundle.js'` specifies the name of the output file, while `path: path.resolve(__dirname, 'dist')` defines the directory where the bundle will be saved (`dist` in this case).

4.3 Mode

The `mode` option can be set to `development`, `production`, or `none`. In `development` mode, Webpack generates a non-minified bundle with helpful comments for debugging. In `production` mode, Webpack performs a series of optimizations to reduce the bundle size, such as minification and tree-shaking.

4.4 Running Webpack

Now that Webpack is configured, you can run the command to generate the bundle:

```bash
npx webpack
```

After running this command, Webpack will generate the `bundle.js` file in the `dist` folder. You can then link this file in your `index.html`:

```html
<!DOCTYPE html>
<html lang="en">
<head>
  <meta charset="UTF-8">
```

```
    <meta name="viewport" content="width=device-width, initial-scale=1.0">
    <title>My Webpack Project</title>
</head>
<body>
    <script src="./dist/bundle.js"></script>
</body>
</html>
```

By opening the `index.html` file in a browser, you will see the output of your Webpack project.

3. Fundamental Webpack Concepts

Webpack is a bundling and optimization tool for modern JavaScript applications, helping manage the increasing complexity of frontend development. With Webpack, you can create code bundles, manage static assets, load various types of modules, and apply optimizations to enhance application performance. In this guide, we will explore the fundamental concepts of Webpack, including modules, modularity, module types, entry points, output, loaders, and plugins.

1. Modules and Modularity

1.1 What is a Module?

A module is a self-contained block of code that performs a specific function and can be reused in different parts of an application. In the context of Webpack, a module can be a JavaScript file, a CSS file, an image, a font, or even an HTML file. Modularity is a fundamental principle of software development, as it promotes separation of concerns, code maintainability, and reusability.

1.1.1 Example of a JavaScript Module

A simple example of a JavaScript module might be:

```javascript
// math.js
export function add(a, b) {
  return a + b;
}


export function subtract(a, b) {
  return a - b;
```

```
}
```

In this example, `math.js` is a module that exports two functions: `add` and `subtract`. These functions can be imported and used in other modules.

1.1.2 Using the Module in Another Part of the Code

```javascript
// app.js
import { add, subtract } from './math.js';

console.log(add(5, 3)); // Output: 8
console.log(subtract(5, 3)); // Output: 2
```

In `app.js`, we import the `add` and `subtract` functions from the `math.js` module and use them to perform arithmetic operations. This approach modularizes the code and allows for better organization of functionalities within an application.

1.2 Modularity in Webpack

Webpack leverages modularity to build the application's dependency graph. This graph is a representation of the interconnections between modules: Webpack starts from an entry file (entry point) and follows all dependencies, including them in the final bundle.

2. Types of Modules

One of Webpack's strengths is its ability to handle different types of modules. In addition to JavaScript files, Webpack can manage CSS, images, fonts, HTML files, and more. This is made possible through **loaders**, which transform files into modules that Webpack can understand and include in the bundle.

2.1 JavaScript Modules

JavaScript modules are the most common type of module in Webpack. They are used to structure and organize JavaScript code into smaller, reusable parts. Webpack supports both ES6 (ESM) modules and CommonJS modules.

2.1.1 Example of an ES6 Module

```javascript
// greeting.js
export function greet(name) {
  return `Hello, ${name}!`;
}
```

```
```

```javascript
// app.js
import { greet } from './greeting.js';

console.log(greet('Webpack')); // Output: Hello, Webpack!
```

In this example, `greet` is a function exported from `greeting.js` and imported into `app.js`.

2.1.2 CommonJS Modules

Webpack also supports CommonJS modules, which use `module.exports` and `require()` to manage dependencies.

```javascript
// math.js
module.exports = {
  add: function(a, b) {
    return a + b;
  },
  subtract: function(a, b) {
    return a - b;
  }
};
```

```javascript
// app.js
const math = require('./math.js');

console.log(math.add(2, 3)); // Output: 5
```

CommonJS is the standard used in Node.js, while ES6 is the modern standard for JavaScript modules.

2.2 CSS Modules

In addition to JavaScript, Webpack can manage CSS files as modules. This means you can import CSS files directly into JavaScript files. Webpack uses `style-loader` and `css-loader` to include CSS files in the bundle.

2.2.1 Example of a CSS Module

First, you need to install the necessary loaders:

```bash
npm install --save-dev style-loader css-loader
```

Then, configure Webpack to handle CSS files:

```javascript
// webpack.config.js
module.exports = {
  module: {
    rules: [
      {
        test: /\.css$/,
        use: ['style-loader', 'css-loader'],
      },
    ],
  },
};
```

With this configuration, you can import CSS

files into your JavaScript modules:

```javascript
// style.css
body {
  background-color: lightblue;
}


// app.js
import './style.css';


console.log('Webpack is styling your app!');
```

When you run Webpack, the CSS file will be included in the bundle and applied to the HTML document.

2.3 Image Modules

Webpack can also manage assets like images, SVG files, fonts, and more. To do this, specific loaders like `file-loader` or `url-loader` are used.

2.3.1 Example of an Image Module

To manage images, you can use `file-loader`:

```bash
npm install --save-dev file-loader
```

Then, add a rule to handle images in Webpack's configuration file:

```javascript
// webpack.config.js
```

```
module.exports = {
  module: {
    rules: [
      {
        test: /\.(png|svg|jpg|jpeg|gif)$/i,
        type: 'asset/resource',
      },
    ],
  },
};
```

Now you can import images into your JavaScript modules:

```javascript
// app.js
import logo from './logo.png';
```

```
const img = document.createElement('img');
img.src = logo;
document.body.appendChild(img);
```

In this way, Webpack will include the image in the bundle and generate the correct URL for use in the HTML.

2.4 Modules for Fonts and Other Assets

Similar to images, Webpack can handle fonts and other static assets using specific loaders. For example, you can manage fonts with `file-loader` in the same way as images.

```javascript
// webpack.config.js
```

```js
module.exports = {
  module: {
    rules: [
      {
        test: /\.(woff|woff2|eot|ttf|otf)$/i,
        type: 'asset/resource',
      },
    ],
  },
};
```

With this configuration, you can import fonts into your CSS files:

```css
@font-face {
  font-family: 'MyFont';
```

```
  src: url('./myfont.woff2') format('woff2');
  font-weight: normal;
  font-style: normal;
}

body {
  font-family: 'MyFont', sans-serif;
}
```

3. Entry and Output

Entry points and output are two fundamental concepts in Webpack's configuration. The entry point tells Webpack which file or modules to use as the starting point for the dependency graph, while the output specifies where and how Webpack should generate the final bundle.

3.1 Entry Point

The entry point is the main entry point of the application. Webpack starts from this file and follows all dependencies to build the module graph. It can be a single file or a set of files.

3.1.1 Example of a Single Entry Point

```javascript
// webpack.config.js
module.exports = {
  entry: './src/index.js',
  output: {
    filename: 'bundle.js',
    path: path.resolve(__dirname, 'dist'),
  },
};
```

```

In this example, `./src/index.js` is the application's entry point. Webpack will follow all dependencies from this file and include them in the `bundle.js` bundle.

##### **3.1.2 Multiple Entry Points**

For more complex applications, you can configure Webpack with multiple entry points, generating multiple bundles.

```javascript
// webpack.config.js
module.exports = {
  entry: {
    app: './src/app.js',
    admin: './src/admin.js',
  },

```
  output: {
    filename: '[name].bundle.js',
    path: path.resolve(__dirname, 'dist'),
  },
};
```

With this configuration, Webpack will generate two separate bundles: `app.bundle.js` and `admin.bundle.js`, each corresponding to its own entry point.

3.2 Output

The output defines where Webpack should generate the bundles and with what names. The `filename` option allows you to specify the names of the output files, while `path` defines the destination directory.

3.2.1 Example of Output Configuration

```javascript
// webpack.config.js
const path = require('path');

module.exports = {
  entry: './src/index.js',
  output: {
    filename: 'bundle.js',
    path: path.resolve(__dirname, 'dist'),
  },
};
```

In this example, the bundle will be generated in the `dist` directory with the name `bundle.js`.

3.2.2 Multiple Outputs

When using multiple entry points, you can use templates in the output file name:

```javascript
// webpack.config.js
const path = require('path');

module.exports = {
  entry: {
    app: './src/app.js',
    admin: './src/admin.js',
  },
  output: {
    filename: '[name].[contenthash].js',
    path: path.resolve(__dirname, 'dist'),
```

```
    },
};
```

In this case, Webpack will generate `app.[contenthash].js` and `admin.[contenthash].js`, where `[contenthash]` is a unique hash based on the content of the file, useful for cache busting.

4. Loaders

Loaders in Webpack are transformations applied to the source code of modules. They allow you to preprocess files before including them in the bundle. Loaders are particularly useful for managing non-JavaScript files like CSS, images, fonts, and HTML.

4.1 What is a Loader?

A loader is a function that takes the source code of a module and transforms it into another format. Webpack uses loaders to handle different file types and compile languages like TypeScript or SCSS into JavaScript and CSS.

4.2 Common Loaders

There are several commonly used loaders in Webpack:

- **`babel-loader`**: Transpiles ES6+ JavaScript to ES5 for older browser compatibility.

- **`css-loader`**: Resolves CSS imports and dependencies.

- **`style-loader`**: Injects CSS into the DOM.

- **`file-loader`**: Manages image and font files, copying them to the output directory.

- **`url-loader`**: Converts small files to

Base64 URIs to include them directly in the bundle.

- **`html-loader`**: Exports HTML as a string, resolving images and other assets in the process.

4.2.1 Example of Using Loaders

To use `babel-loader` to transpile modern JavaScript, you would:

1. Install Babel and the necessary presets:

```bash
npm install --save-dev babel-loader @babel/core @babel/preset-env
```

2. Configure Webpack to use `babel-loader`:

```javascript
// webpack.config.js
module.exports = {
  module: {
    rules: [
      {
        test: /\.js$/,
        exclude: /node_modules/,
        use: {
          loader: 'babel-loader',
          options: {
            presets: ['@babel/preset-env'],
          },
        },
      },
    ],
  },
};
```

```

With this configuration, Webpack will transpile modern JavaScript syntax into a format compatible with older browsers.

### **5. Plugins**

Plugins are an advanced feature in Webpack that extend its capabilities. Unlike loaders, which transform specific types of modules, plugins can affect the entire build process. They can perform tasks such as optimizing bundles, injecting environment variables, or even generating HTML files.

#### **5.1 What is a Plugin?**

A plugin is a class that implements the `apply` method and hooks into the Webpack compilation process. Plugins can be used to perform a variety of tasks, such as:
```

- **Bundle optimization**: Minifying JavaScript or CSS files.

- **Asset management**: Injecting assets like CSS or JS into HTML.

- **Environment variables**: Defining global constants.

- **Code splitting**: Breaking the codebase into smaller bundles for better performance.

5.2 Common Plugins

Some common plugins in Webpack include:

- **`HtmlWebpackPlugin`**: Simplifies the creation of HTML files to serve bundles.

- **`MiniCssExtractPlugin`**: Extracts CSS into separate files.

- **`DefinePlugin`**: Creates global constants, typically used for environment variables.

- **`CleanWebpackPlugin`**: Removes old files from the output directory before each build.

- **`TerserPlugin`**: Minifies JavaScript to reduce bundle size.

5.2.1 Example of Using a Plugin

To use `HtmlWebpackPlugin` to generate an HTML file that includes all your bundles:

1. Install the plugin:

```bash
npm install --save-dev html-webpack-plugin
```

2. Add the plugin to the Webpack configuration:

```javascript
// webpack.config.js
const HtmlWebpackPlugin = require('html-webpack-plugin');

module.exports = {
  plugins: [
    new HtmlWebpackPlugin({
      title: 'My App',
      template: './src/index.html',
    }),
  ],
};
```

With this configuration, Webpack will generate an `index.html` file in the output directory that automatically includes all bundles.

6. Putting it All Together

A comprehensive Webpack configuration that brings together entry points, outputs, loaders, and plugins might look like this:

```javascript
// webpack.config.js
const path = require('path');
const HtmlWebpackPlugin = require('html-webpack-plugin');
const MiniCssExtractPlugin = require('mini-css-extract-plugin');

module.exports = {
  entry: './src/index.js',
  output: {
    filename: 'bundle.[contenthash].js',
    path: path.resolve(__dirname, 'dist'),
```

```
    clean: true, // Clean the output directory before each build
  },
  module: {
    rules: [
      {
        test: /\.js$/,
        exclude: /node_modules/,
        use: 'babel-loader',
      },
      {
        test: /\.css$/,
        use: [MiniCssExtractPlugin.loader, 'css-loader'],
      },
      {
        test: /\.(png|svg|jpg|jpeg|gif)$/i,
        type: 'asset/resource',
      },
```

```
    ],
  },
  plugins: [
    new HtmlWebpackPlugin({
      template: './src/index.html',
    }),
    new MiniCssExtractPlugin({
      filename: '[name].[contenthash].css',
    }),
  ],
  mode: 'production', // Set the mode to production for optimized builds
};
```

This configuration includes:

- An entry point at `./src/index.js`.

- Output configuration with content hash for cache busting.

- Loaders for JavaScript (using Babel), CSS, and image files.

- Plugins to generate an HTML file, extract CSS, and clean the output directory.

7. Conclusion

Understanding the fundamental concepts of Webpack, such as modules, entry points, outputs, loaders, and plugins, is crucial for efficiently bundling and optimizing modern web applications. Webpack's flexibility allows it to handle various types of assets and perform complex build processes, making it a powerful tool in the frontend developer's toolkit. With this knowledge, you can start configuring Webpack to suit the needs of your specific project, enabling a more organized, maintainable, and performant codebase.

4. Webpack Loaders

1. Introduction to Loaders

Loaders in Webpack are essential tools that allow Webpack to handle and transform different types of files, beyond just JavaScript files. In other words, a loader enables Webpack to process file types that it cannot interpret natively, converting them into modules that can be included in the final bundle.

By default, Webpack is designed to handle JavaScript files, but with loaders, Webpack's capabilities can be extended to handle any type of file, such as CSS, images, fonts, JSON files, and much more. Loaders are configured in the Webpack configuration file and applied using **rules** that specify which files should be transformed and with which loaders.

2. How Loaders Work

Loaders in Webpack are essentially functions that take a file as input and return a modified version of that file, allowing Webpack to manage it within its dependency graph. This process enables, for example, the transformation of CSS files into JavaScript modules or the conversion of ES6+ files into ES5 code that is compatible with older browsers.

When configuring a loader, it's important to define a few properties:

- **test**: A regex that defines which files should be processed by the loader.

- **use**: Specifies the loader or loaders to be applied to those files.

- **exclude**: Excludes certain files or directories from being processed.

- **include**: Limits processing to specific files or directories.

3. Configuring Commonly Used Loaders

There are several commonly used loaders in Webpack, each catering to specific development needs. Below, we'll explore the configuration and usage of some of the most popular loaders: `babel-loader`, `css-loader`, `style-loader`, `file-loader`, and `url-loader`.

3.1 Babel Loader

`babel-loader` is one of the most widely used loaders for transforming modern JavaScript (ES6+) into code compatible with all browsers, including older ones. Babel is a JavaScript transpiler, and the Webpack loader for Babel allows this transformation process to be integrated into the Webpack workflow.

3.1.1 Installing Babel and Babel Loader

To use `babel-loader`, you need to install Babel along with the necessary presets:

```bash
npm install --save-dev babel-loader @babel/core @babel/preset-env
```

`@babel/core` is the core engine of Babel, while `@babel/preset-env` is a preset that automatically handles the transformation of JavaScript code based on the target browsers.

3.1.2 Configuring Babel Loader

In the Webpack configuration file (`webpack.config.js`), you can configure `babel-loader` as follows:

```javascript
```

```js
// webpack.config.js
module.exports = {
  module: {
    rules: [
      {
        test: /\.js$/, // Transforms all .js files
        exclude: /node_modules/, // Excludes the node_modules folder
        use: {
          loader: 'babel-loader',
          options: {
            presets: ['@babel/preset-env'], // Uses the preset-env
          },
        },
      },
    ],
  },
};
```

```

This configuration ensures that every `.js` file is transformed by Babel, except those in the `node_modules` folder.

##### **3.1.3 Example of Transformed Code**

If your project includes a JavaScript file using ES6+ syntax, such as:

```javascript
// src/app.js
const greet = (name) => {
  console.log(`Hello, ${name}!`);
};

greet('World');

```

`babel-loader` will transform the code into an ES5-compatible version:

```javascript
// Transformed by Babel
"use strict";

var greet = function greet(name) {
  console.log("Hello, " + name + "!");
};

greet('World');
```

3.2 CSS Loader and Style Loader

CSS is an essential part of any web application, and Webpack can handle CSS
```

files as modules thanks to `css-loader` and `style-loader`. While `css-loader` allows Webpack to interpret CSS files and manage CSS imports, `style-loader` injects these styles into the DOM during runtime.

3.2.1 Installing CSS Loader and Style Loader

To use `css-loader` and `style-loader`, you need to install them via npm:

```bash
npm install --save-dev css-loader style-loader
```

3.2.2 Configuring CSS Loader and Style Loader

The typical configuration to handle CSS files is as follows:

```javascript
// webpack.config.js
module.exports = {
  module: {
    rules: [
      {
        test: /\.css$/, // Transforms all .css files
        use: ['style-loader', 'css-loader'], // Applies css-loader first, then style-loader
      },
    ],
  },
};
```

With this configuration, every time you import a CSS file into your JavaScript files, Webpack will automatically handle the CSS.

3.2.3 Usage Example

You can import a CSS file in a JavaScript module as follows:

```javascript
// src/styles.css
body {
  background-color: lightblue;
  font-family: Arial, sans-serif;
}

// src/index.js
import './styles.css';

console.log('Styles have been applied!');
```

When you run Webpack, `style-loader` will inject the CSS into the DOM, applying the styles defined in the `styles.css` file.

3.3 File Loader

`file-loader` is a useful loader for handling assets like images, fonts, and other files. The loader resolves the paths of these assets and copies them to the output directory, returning the URL for accessing the file.

3.3.1 Installing File Loader

To use `file-loader`, you need to install it via npm:

```bash
npm install --save-dev file-loader
```

3.3.2 Configuring File Loader

The basic configuration for `file-loader` is quite simple:

```javascript
// webpack.config.js
module.exports = {
  module: {
    rules: [
      {
        test: /\.(png|jpg|gif|svg)$/, // Transforms images and SVG files
        use: {
          loader: 'file-loader',
          options: {
            name: '[name].[hash].[ext]', // Keeps the file name and adds a hash
```

```
        outputPath: 'images/', // Saves files in the "images" folder
      },
    },
   },
  ],
 },
};
```

3.3.3 Usage Example

You can import an image in your JavaScript module:

```javascript
// src/image.js
import logo from './logo.png';
```

```js
const img = document.createElement('img');
img.src = logo;
document.body.appendChild(img);
```

`file-loader` will handle the `logo.png` file, copy it to the `images/` folder (with a unique hash to avoid conflicts), and return the URL to access the image.

3.4 URL Loader

`url-loader` is similar to `file-loader`, but with an added feature: if the file is smaller than a certain size (defined in bytes), `url-loader` can convert it into a Base64 URL, directly embedding the file into the JavaScript bundle.

3.4.1 Installing URL Loader

To use `url-loader`, you need to install it via npm:

```bash
npm install --save-dev url-loader
```

3.4.2 Configuring URL Loader

The configuration for `url-loader` might look similar to that of `file-loader`, but with an additional option:

```javascript
// webpack.config.js
module.exports = {
  module: {
    rules: [
      {
```

```
      test: /\.(png|jpg|gif|svg)$/, // Transforms images and SVG files
      use: {
        loader: 'url-loader',
        options: {
          limit: 8192, // Embeds files smaller than 8kb
          name: '[name].[hash].[ext]', // Keeps the file name and adds a hash
          outputPath: 'images/', // Saves files in the "images" folder
        },
      },
    },
  ],
 },
};
```

If a file is smaller than 8kb, it will be embedded as a Base64 URL. Otherwise, `url-loader` will behave like `file-loader`.

3.4.3 Usage Example

The usage is identical to `file-loader`, with the difference that small files will be directly embedded into the JavaScript code as Base64 strings, reducing the number of HTTP requests.

4. Writing and Registering a Custom Loader

One of the most powerful aspects of Webpack is the ability to create and use custom loaders. A custom loader is simply a JavaScript function that takes a file as input and returns a modified version of the file as output.

4.1 Creating a Custom Loader

Suppose you want to create a loader that converts all the text in a JavaScript file to uppercase. Here's how you might do it:

4.1.1 Loader Structure

A loader is a function that receives the content of the file as input (in the form of a string or buffer) and returns the transformed content:

```javascript
// uppercase-loader.js
module.exports = function (source) {
  return source.toUpperCase();
};
```

This loader transforms all the content of the file into uppercase.

4.2 Registering the Loader

Once the loader is created, you can use it in your Webpack project. Suppose you want to apply this loader to all `.txt` files:

4.2.1 Webpack Configuration

In the Webpack configuration file (`webpack.config.js`), you can configure the custom loader as follows:

```javascript
// webpack.config.js
const path = require('path');
```

```js
module.exports = {
  module: {
    rules: [
      {
        test: /\.txt$/, // Applies the loader to .txt files
        use: path.resolve(__dirname, 'uppercase-loader.js'), // Path to the custom loader
      },
    ],
  },
};
```

4.2.2 Usage Example

Now you can import a `.txt` file in a JavaScript module:

```javascript
// src/index.js
import content from './sample.txt';

console.log(content); // All text will be in uppercase
```

If the `sample.txt` file contains:

```
Hello, World!
```

The custom loader will transform it into:

```
HELLO, WORLD!
```

```

And this will be the result visible in the browser.

### **5. Conclusion**

Webpack loaders are incredibly powerful tools that extend Webpack's functionality to handle any type of file, transforming them into JavaScript modules. Whether you're working with modern JavaScript, CSS, images, fonts, or even text files, there's a loader that can help you easily integrate these files into your project.

Moreover, the ability to create custom loaders offers an unprecedented level of flexibility and control, allowing you to tailor Webpack completely to the specific needs of your project. Whether you're using common loaders like `babel-loader`, `css-loader`, `file-loader`, or `url-loader`, or creating your own
```

from scratch, understanding how they work and how to configure them is essential to fully leveraging Webpack's potential.

With an in-depth understanding of loaders and their configuration, you'll be able to build modular, scalable, and optimized web applications for any deployment context, while maintaining complete control over the build process.

5. Webpack Plugins

Plugins in Webpack extend Webpack's basic capabilities and offer advanced control over the build process. While **loaders** are used to transform files into modules that Webpack can manage, plugins operate on a higher level, interacting with the build process to perform more complex and customized operations.

A plugin in Webpack is essentially a JavaScript class that implements one or more specific methods, known as hooks, which Webpack calls during its compilation lifecycle. Plugins can manipulate bundles, optimize assets, generate additional files, and much more. Using plugins allows you to customize Webpack's behavior to meet the specific needs of a project.

2. How Plugins Work

Plugins in Webpack integrate into the Webpack build lifecycle through a system of hooks. These hooks are specific points where plugins can execute their code. Plugins can use these hooks to access and modify various aspects of the build.

2.1 Common Plugin Hooks

Here are some of the main hooks that plugins can use:

- **`compilation`**: Executed at the start of the compilation phase. It allows access to and modification of the compilation and modules.

- **`emit`**: Executed when Webpack is ready to emit files. It allows modification of files before they are written to disk.

- **`done`**: Executed at the end of the build process. Useful for performing final operations, such as generating reports or sending notifications.

3. Configuring Commonly Used Plugins

Let's take a look at how to configure some of the most commonly used plugins in Webpack: `HtmlWebpackPlugin`, `MiniCssExtractPlugin`, and `CleanWebpackPlugin`.

3.1 HtmlWebpackPlugin

`HtmlWebpackPlugin` is a fundamental plugin for automatically generating HTML files that include your JavaScript bundles. This plugin is useful for avoiding manual updates to HTML files whenever the bundles change.

3.1.1 Installing HtmlWebpackPlugin

To install `HtmlWebpackPlugin`, run the

following command:

```bash
npm install --save-dev html-webpack-plugin
```

3.1.2 Configuring HtmlWebpackPlugin

Here is a basic configuration example:

```javascript
// webpack.config.js
const HtmlWebpackPlugin = require('html-webpack-plugin');

module.exports = {
  plugins: [
    new HtmlWebpackPlugin({
```

```
      title: 'My App', // Title of the HTML page
      template: './src/index.html', // HTML template to use
      filename: 'index.html', // Name of the generated HTML file
    }),
  ],
};
```

In this example, `HtmlWebpackPlugin` uses `index.html` as the template and generates an `index.html` file in the output directory, automatically including your JavaScript bundles.

3.1.3 Additional Options for HtmlWebpackPlugin

`HtmlWebpackPlugin` offers several additional options:

- **`inject`**: Specifies where to insert script and link tags. It can be `true`, `body`, `head`, or `false`.

- **`minify`**: Options for minimizing the HTML file, such as removing whitespace and comments.

- **`meta`**: Adds metadata to the HTML document.

Advanced configuration example:

```javascript
new HtmlWebpackPlugin({
  title: 'My Optimized App',
  template: './src/index.html',
  filename: 'index.html',
  minify: {
    collapseWhitespace: true, // Removes whitespace
```

```
    removeComments: true, // Removes comments

    removeRedundantAttributes: true, // Removes redundant attributes
  },
  meta: {
    viewport: 'width=device-width, initial-scale=1',
  },
});
```

3.2 MiniCssExtractPlugin

`MiniCssExtractPlugin` is used to extract CSS from JavaScript files and generate separate CSS files. This plugin is particularly useful for asynchronously loading CSS and improving loading performance.

3.2.1 Installing MiniCssExtractPlugin

To install `MiniCssExtractPlugin`, run:

```bash
npm install --save-dev mini-css-extract-plugin css-loader
```

3.2.2 Configuring MiniCssExtractPlugin

Here is an example configuration:

```javascript
// webpack.config.js
const MiniCssExtractPlugin = require('mini-css-extract-plugin');
```

```
module.exports = {
  module: {
    rules: [
      {
        test: /\.css$/, // Applies the loader to .css files
        use: [MiniCssExtractPlugin.loader, 'css-loader'], // Extracts CSS and transforms it into modules
      },
    ],
  },
  plugins: [
    new MiniCssExtractPlugin({
      filename: '[name].[contenthash].css', // Name of the generated CSS file
    }),
  ],
```

};
```

In this example, `MiniCssExtractPlugin` extracts the CSS into a separate file with a name that includes a content hash, which is useful for caching.

##### **3.2.3 Usage Example**

In your JavaScript file, you can import CSS as follows:

```javascript
// src/index.js
import './styles.css';
```

When you run Webpack, `MiniCssExtractPlugin` will create a separate
```

CSS file for your stylesheet.

3.3 CleanWebpackPlugin

`CleanWebpackPlugin` is used to clean the output directory (e.g., `dist/`) before generating new files, preventing the accumulation of outdated files.

3.3.1 Installing CleanWebpackPlugin

To install `CleanWebpackPlugin`, run:

```bash
npm install --save-dev clean-webpack-plugin
```

3.3.2 Configuring CleanWebpackPlugin

Here's how to configure `CleanWebpackPlugin`:

```javascript
// webpack.config.js
const { CleanWebpackPlugin } = require('clean-webpack-plugin');

module.exports = {
  plugins: [
    new CleanWebpackPlugin(), // Cleans the dist/ folder before each build
  ],
};
```

This configuration ensures that the `dist/` folder is cleaned before each build, preventing the accumulation of outdated files.

3.3.3 Additional Options for CleanWebpackPlugin

`CleanWebpackPlugin` offers several options for customizing its behavior:

- **`cleanOnceBeforeBuildPatterns`**: An array of patterns for the files to be removed.

- **`cleanStaleWebpackAssets`**: If set to `true`, removes stale assets that are no longer used.

- **`protectWebpackAssets`**: If set to `true`, prevents the accidental removal of assets.

Advanced configuration example:

```javascript
new CleanWebpackPlugin({
  cleanOnceBeforeBuildPatterns: ['**/*', '!
```

static-files*'], // Removes everything except static files

  cleanStaleWebpackAssets: true,

  protectWebpackAssets: false,

});
```

### **4. Writing and Using a Custom Plugin**

Creating a custom plugin in Webpack allows you to add specific functionality that is not covered by existing plugins. A custom plugin can be used to perform unique operations during the Webpack build lifecycle.

#### **4.1 Creating a Custom Plugin**

Suppose you want to create a plugin that logs a message to the console every time the Webpack build is completed.
```

4.1.1 Writing the Plugin

Here's an example of a custom plugin:

```javascript
// my-custom-plugin.js
class MyCustomPlugin {
  apply(compiler) {
    // Hook executed at the end of the compilation
    compiler.hooks.done.tap('MyCustomPlugin', (stats) => {
      console.log('The Webpack build is complete!');
    });
  }
}
```

```
module.exports = MyCustomPlugin;
```

In this example, the plugin uses the `done` hook to print a message to the console when the build is complete.

4.2 Using the Custom Plugin

To use the custom plugin, you need to register it in the Webpack configuration file:

```javascript
// webpack.config.js
const MyCustomPlugin = require('./my-custom-plugin');

module.exports = {
```

```
  plugins: [
    new MyCustomPlugin(), // Add your custom plugin
  ],
};
```

When you run a build with this configuration, you will see the console message every time Webpack completes the build process.

4.3 Advanced Options for Custom Plugins

Webpack plugins can be much more complex, interacting with various hooks and stages of the build process. Here are some advanced hooks you might want to use:

- **`compilation`**: This hook is executed during the compilation phase, allowing you to modify the dependency graph.

- **`emit`**: Executed before files are written to disk, useful for manipulating output files.

- **`afterEmit`**: Executed after files have been written to disk, useful for performing post-build operations.

Example using multiple hooks:

```javascript
class AdvancedPlugin {
  apply(compiler) {

    compiler.hooks.compilation.tap('AdvancedPlugin', (compilation) => {
      console.log('Compilation started!');
    });


    compiler.hooks.emit.tapAsync('AdvancedPlug
```

```
in', (compilation, callback) => {
    console.log('Files are being written...');
    callback(); // Pass to the next hook
  });

  compiler.hooks.done.tap('AdvancedPlugin', (stats) => {
    console.log('The Webpack build is complete!');
  });
  }
}

module.exports = AdvancedPlugin;
```

Webpack plugins offer great flexibility to extend and customize the build process. Whether you are using standard plugins like `HtmlWebpackPlugin`,

`MiniCssExtractPlugin`, and `CleanWebpackPlugin`, or creating custom plugins for specific needs, it is essential to understand how plugins interact with the Webpack lifecycle and how to configure them to achieve the best results.

Properly configuring plugins can significantly improve the performance, quality, and management of your project's builds, making the development and deployment process more efficient and tailored to your specific needs. Whether automating repetitive tasks, optimizing assets, or implementing custom functionality, Webpack plugins provide the necessary flexibility to build and manage modern and complex web projects.

6. Development and Production Modes in Webpack

Webpack is a powerful tool for managing and building JavaScript projects, and its configuration can vary significantly between development and production environments. Properly configuring Webpack for each of these modes is crucial for achieving an efficient workflow during development and ensuring optimal performance and minified code in production.

Development-Specific Configurations

During development, it's essential to have a configuration that favors compilation speed and provides immediate feedback on errors. Development configurations tend to prioritize ease of use and speed over performance optimizations.

1.1 Basic Development Configuration

Here is an example of a basic configuration for a development environment:

```javascript
// webpack.dev.js
const path = require('path');
const HtmlWebpackPlugin = require('html-webpack-plugin');
const webpack = require('webpack');

module.exports = {
  mode: 'development',
  entry: './src/index.js',
  output: {
    filename: 'bundle.js',
    path: path.resolve(__dirname, 'dist'),
    publicPath: '/',
  },
```

```
devtool: 'inline-source-map', // Enables source map for easier debugging
devServer: {
  contentBase: path.join(__dirname, 'dist'),
  compress: true,
  port: 9000,
  hot: true, // Enables hot module replacement
},
plugins: [
  new HtmlWebpackPlugin({
    template: './src/index.html',
  }),
  new webpack.HotModuleReplacementPlugin(), // Plugin for hot module replacement
],
module: {
  rules: [
```

```
      {
        test: /\.css$/,
        use: ['style-loader', 'css-loader'], // Uses style-loader and css-loader for CSS
      },
    ],
  },
};
```

Explanation of Settings:

- **`mode: 'development'`**: Sets Webpack to development mode, which disables certain automatic optimizations.

- **`devtool: 'inline-source-map'`**: Generates inline source maps for easier debugging.

- **`devServer`**: Configures Webpack's built-in development server with support for hot reloading and compression.

- **`plugins`**: Uses `HtmlWebpackPlugin` to generate an HTML file and `HotModuleReplacementPlugin` for hot module replacement.

Production-Specific Configurations

In production, the focus is on code optimization and minimization to improve performance. Production configuration typically includes JavaScript and CSS minimization, extracting CSS into separate files, and managing static assets.

2.1 Basic Production Configuration

Here is an example of a basic configuration for a production environment:

```javascript
```

```js
// webpack.prod.js
const path = require('path');
const MiniCssExtractPlugin = require('mini-css-extract-plugin');
const TerserPlugin = require('terser-webpack-plugin');
const OptimizeCSSAssetsPlugin = require('optimize-css-assets-webpack-plugin');
const HtmlWebpackPlugin = require('html-webpack-plugin');
const { CleanWebpackPlugin } = require('clean-webpack-plugin');


module.exports = {
  mode: 'production',
  entry: './src/index.js',
  output: {
    filename: '[name].[contenthash].js',
    path: path.resolve(__dirname, 'dist'),
    publicPath: '/',
```

```
  },
  devtool: 'source-map', // Enables source map for debugging
  plugins: [
    new CleanWebpackPlugin(), // Cleans the output folder
    new HtmlWebpackPlugin({
      template: './src/index.html',
      minify: {
        collapseWhitespace: true,
        removeComments: true,
      },
    }),
    new MiniCssExtractPlugin({
      filename: '[name].[contenthash].css',
    }),
  ],
  optimization: {
    minimize: true,
```

```
      minimizer: [
        new TerserPlugin(), // Minimizes JavaScript
        new OptimizeCSSAssetsPlugin(), // Minimizes CSS
      ],
    },
    module: {
      rules: [
        {
          test: /\.css$/,
          use: [MiniCssExtractPlugin.loader, 'css-loader'],
        },
        {
          test: /\.(png|jpg|gif|svg)$/,
          use: [
            {
              loader: 'file-loader',
```

```
          options: {
            name: '[path][name].[ext]',
            outputPath: 'assets/',
          },
        },
      ],
    },
   ],
  },
};
```

Explanation of Settings:

- **`mode: 'production'`**: Sets Webpack to production mode, activating optimizations like code minimization.

- **`devtool: 'source-map'`**: Generates external source maps for production debugging.

- **`plugins`**: Uses `MiniCssExtractPlugin` to extract CSS into separate files, `CleanWebpackPlugin` to clean the output directory, and `HtmlWebpackPlugin` to optimize HTML.

- **`optimization`**: Configures minimization for JavaScript and CSS.

Enabling Source Maps

Source maps are essential for debugging, as they map compiled code back to the original source code. Webpack supports various source map modes, which affect the quality and speed of map generation.

3.1 Source Map Modes

- **`source-map`**: Creates a separate file for the source map, ideal for production.

- **`inline-source-map`**: Inserts the source map directly into the JavaScript file, useful for development.

- **`eval-source-map`**: Uses `eval()` to generate inline source maps, faster but less secure.

- **`cheap-module-source-map`**: Provides less detailed source maps that are faster to generate, suitable for production.

3.2 Enabling Source Maps in Configuration

To enable source maps in Webpack, simply set the `devtool` option in the configuration:

```javascript
// webpack.config.js
module.exports = {
  devtool: 'source-map', // Enables source maps in production
};
```

```

### Performance Optimization in Production

Production optimizations aim to reduce file sizes, improve loading times, and ensure a smooth user experience. Key optimizations include minimization, static asset management, and code splitting.

#### 4.1 Minimization

Minimizing JavaScript and CSS code reduces file sizes and improves loading times. Use plugins like `TerserPlugin` for JavaScript and `OptimizeCSSAssetsPlugin` for CSS.

##### **Example of Minimization**

```javascript

```
// webpack.prod.js
const TerserPlugin = require('terser-webpack-plugin');
const OptimizeCSSAssetsPlugin = require('optimize-css-assets-webpack-plugin');

module.exports = {
  optimization: {
    minimize: true,
    minimizer: [
      new TerserPlugin(), // Minimizes JavaScript
      new OptimizeCSSAssetsPlugin(), // Minimizes CSS
    ],
  },
};
```

4.2 Code Splitting

Code splitting divides code into multiple files, loading them only when necessary. Use `import()` to split bundles and `SplitChunksPlugin` to manage common files.

Example of Code Splitting

```javascript
// webpack.config.js
module.exports = {
  optimization: {
    splitChunks: {
      chunks: 'all', // Splits all chunks into separate files
    },
  },
};
```

```

#### 4.3 Lazy Loading

Lazy loading loads modules only when they are needed, reducing initial loading time. Use `import()` to implement lazy loading.

##### **Example of Lazy Loading**

```javascript
// src/index.js
import(/* webpackChunkName: "moduleA" */ './moduleA').then(module => {
  // Use the loaded module
});
```

Debugging and Troubleshooting
```

Debugging Webpack can be complex, but with the right techniques and tools, it's possible to resolve issues and optimize the configuration.

Common Webpack Errors

Some common Webpack errors include:

- **`ModuleNotFoundError`**: Indicates that Webpack cannot find a specified module. Check the file path and name.

- **`SyntaxError`**: Often caused by syntax errors in the code. Check your source code syntax.

- **`WebpackError`**: General errors that may occur during the build process. Check detailed error logs for more information.

Debugging Techniques

6.1 Using Webpack Logs

Webpack logs provide useful details on errors and warnings. Set the log level to get more detailed information.

Example of Log Configuration

```javascript
// webpack.config.js
module.exports = {
  stats: 'verbose', // Provides detailed output
};
```

6.2 Enabling Loader Debugging

Loaders can generate specific errors. Enable

logging for loaders to diagnose issues.

Example of Loader Configuration

```javascript
// webpack.config.js
module.exports = {
  module: {
    rules: [
      {
        test: /\.js$/,
        use: {
          loader: 'babel-loader',
          options: {
            sourceMaps: true, // Enables source maps for loaders
          },
        },
```

```
      },
    ],
  },
};
```

Using Watch Mode for Monitoring Changes

Webpack offers a `watch` mode to monitor files and automatically recompile when changes are made. This mode is useful during development to see changes immediately.

7.1 Enabling Watch Mode

You can enable watch mode via Webpack configuration or from the command line.

**Example of Watch Mode

Configuration**

```javascript
// webpack.config.js
module.exports = {
  watch: true, // Enables watch mode
};
```

Example of Command Line Usage

```bash
npx webpack --watch
```

When Webpack is in watch mode, it automatically recompiles whenever a watched file is modified.

Configuring Webpack for development and production modes requires understanding the specific needs of each environment. Development mode should be optimized for speed and ease of debugging, while production mode should focus on minimization, performance optimization, and asset management. Using source maps, performance optimization techniques, and debugging methods are all essential for ensuring an efficient

and problem-free build process. Effectively leveraging these configurations and techniques will help you get the most out of Webpack and improve the quality and efficiency of your development and deployment processes.

7. Integration with Other Tools in Webpack

Webpack is renowned for its flexibility and its ability to integrate with a wide range of tools and libraries. This section will explore how to integrate Webpack with common tools such as Babel, TypeScript, popular frameworks, and the management of images and static assets. Additionally, we will discuss testing with Webpack and best practices for configuration and optimization.

Integration with Babel

Babel is a JavaScript compiler that allows you to use the latest language features even on browsers that do not natively support them. Webpack can be configured to use Babel to transpile modern JavaScript code into a version compatible with target environments.

**1.1 Configuring Babel with

Webpack**

To integrate Babel with Webpack, you need to install `babel-loader`, `@babel/core`, and the necessary presets. The steps are as follows:

Installation

```bash
npm install --save-dev babel-loader @babel/core @babel/preset-env
```

Webpack Configuration

Add Babel configuration to your Webpack configuration file:

```javascript
```

```js
// webpack.config.js
const path = require('path');

module.exports = {
  entry: './src/index.js',
  output: {
    filename: 'bundle.js',
    path: path.resolve(__dirname, 'dist'),
  },
  module: {
    rules: [
      {
        test: /\.js$/,
        exclude: /node_modules/,
        use: {
          loader: 'babel-loader',
          options: {
            presets: ['@babel/preset-env'], //
```

Configures Babel to use the default preset for ES6+

```
        },
      },
    },
  ],
  },
};
```

Babel Configuration

Create a `.babelrc` file at the root of your project to configure Babel:

```json
{
  "presets": ["@babel/preset-env"]
}
```

```

This configures Babel to transform ECMAScript 2015+ code into a version compatible with older browsers.

#### **1.2 Using Babel Plugins**

You can also add specific plugins for advanced features. For example, to use proposed features like decorators, add the `@babel/plugin-proposal-decorators` plugin:

##### **Installation**

```bash
npm install --save-dev @babel/plugin-proposal-decorators
```
```

Babel Configuration

Update the `.babelrc` file:

```json
{
  "presets": ["@babel/preset-env"],
  "plugins": ["@babel/plugin-proposal-decorators"]
}
```

Integration with TypeScript

TypeScript is a superset of JavaScript that adds static typing. Webpack can be configured to work with TypeScript using either `ts-loader` or `babel-loader`.

2.1 Configuring TypeScript with Webpack

To integrate TypeScript, you need to install `typescript` and `ts-loader`.

Installation

```bash
npm install --save-dev typescript ts-loader
```

Webpack Configuration

Update the Webpack configuration file to support TypeScript:

```javascript
// webpack.config.js
```

```javascript
const path = require('path');

module.exports = {
  entry: './src/index.ts',
  output: {
    filename: 'bundle.js',
    path: path.resolve(__dirname, 'dist'),
  },
  module: {
    rules: [
      {
        test: /\.ts$/,
        exclude: /node_modules/,
        use: 'ts-loader', // Uses ts-loader to handle TypeScript files
      },
    ],
  },
```

```
  resolve: {
    extensions: ['.ts', '.js'], // Resolves .ts and .js files
  },
};
```

TypeScript Configuration

Create a `tsconfig.json` file at the root of your project to configure the TypeScript compiler:

```json
{
  "compilerOptions": {
    "target": "es6",
    "module": "commonjs",
    "outDir": "./dist",
    "rootDir": "./src",
```

```
    "strict": true
  },
  "include": ["src/**/*.ts"],
  "exclude": ["node_modules"]
}
```

This file configures the TypeScript compiler to use ECMAScript 6 as the target and CommonJS as the module system.

Integration with Frameworks

Webpack can be configured to work with popular frameworks like React, Vue, and Angular.

3.1 Integrating with React

To use React with Webpack, you need to install `react`, `react-dom`, and `babel-loader`.

Installation

```bash
npm install --save react react-dom
npm install --save-dev babel-loader @babel/core @babel/preset-react
```

Webpack Configuration

Configure Webpack to support JSX and React:

```javascript
// webpack.config.js
const path = require('path');
```

```javascript
module.exports = {
  entry: './src/index.js',
  output: {
    filename: 'bundle.js',
    path: path.resolve(__dirname, 'dist'),
  },
  module: {
    rules: [
      {
        test: /\.jsx?$/, // Handles .js and .jsx files
        exclude: /node_modules/,
        use: {
          loader: 'babel-loader',
          options: {
            presets: ['@babel/preset-env', '@babel/preset-react'], // Add preset-react
          },
```

```
      },
    },
   ],
  },
  resolve: {
    extensions: ['.js', '.jsx'], // Resolves .js and .jsx files
  },
};
```

Example of a React Component

```javascript
// src/App.jsx
import React from 'react';

const App = () => <h1>Hello, React!</h1>;
```

```
export default App;
```

```javascript
// src/index.js
import React from 'react';
import ReactDOM from 'react-dom';
import App from './App';

ReactDOM.render(<App />, document.getElementById('root'));
```

3.2 Integrating with Vue

To use Vue with Webpack, you need to install `vue` and `vue-loader`.

Installation

```bash
npm install --save vue
npm install --save-dev vue-loader vue-template-compiler
```

Webpack Configuration

Configure Webpack to handle `.vue` files:

```javascript
// webpack.config.js
const path = require('path');
const VueLoaderPlugin = require('vue-loader/lib/plugin');

module.exports = {
```

```
entry: './src/main.js',
output: {
  filename: 'bundle.js',
  path: path.resolve(__dirname, 'dist'),
},
module: {
  rules: [
    {
      test: /\.vue$/,
      loader: 'vue-loader', // Uses vue-loader for .vue files
    },
    {
      test: /\.js$/,
      loader: 'babel-loader',
      exclude: /node_modules/,
    },
  ],
```

},
  plugins: [
    new VueLoaderPlugin(), // Required for vue-loader
  ],
  resolve: {
    alias: {
      vue$: 'vue/dist/vue.runtime.esm.js', // Uses the runtime-only build
    },
    extensions: ['.js', '.vue'],
  },
};
```

##### **Example of a Vue Component**

```html
<!-- src/App.vue -->

```
<template>
  <h1>Hello, Vue!</h1>
</template>

<script>
export default {
  name: 'App',
};
</script>

<style>
h1 {
  color: green;
}
</style>
```

```javascript
```

```
// src/main.js
import Vue from 'vue';
import App from './App.vue';

new Vue({
  render: (h) => h(App),
}).$mount('#app');
```

3.3 Integrating with Angular

Angular has its own CLI that manages Webpack configuration, but you can use Webpack directly if needed.

Installation

If you want to manage Webpack manually, make sure to install the base Angular and

Webpack dependencies:

```bash
npm install --save @angular/core @angular/cli
npm install --save-dev webpack webpack-cli ts-loader
```

Webpack Configuration

Configure Webpack for TypeScript and Angular:

```javascript
// webpack.config.js
const path = require('path');

module.exports = {
```

```
  entry: './src/main.ts',
  output: {
    filename: 'bundle.js',
    path: path.resolve(__dirname, 'dist'),
  },
  module: {
    rules: [
      {
        test: /\.ts$/,
        use: 'ts-loader',
        exclude: /node_modules/,
      },
    ],
  },
  resolve: {
    extensions: ['.ts', '.js'],
  },
};
```

```

### Managing Images and Static Assets

Webpack manages images and other static assets through loaders like `file-loader` and `url-loader`.

#### **4.1 Configuring file-loader and url-loader**

These loaders can be used to handle images and static assets, allowing you to emit files and manage their URLs.

##### **Installation**

```bash
npm install --save-dev file-loader url-loader
```
```

Webpack Configuration

Add a rule to handle images and static assets:

```javascript
// webpack.config.js
const path = require('path');

module.exports = {
  entry: './src/index.js',
  output: {
    filename: 'bundle.js',
    path: path.resolve(__dirname, 'dist'),
  },
  module: {
    rules: [
      {
```

```
        test: /\.(png|jpg|gif|svg)$/,
        use: [
          {
            loader: 'file-loader',
            options: {
              name: '[name].[ext]',
              outputPath: 'images/', // Save images in the 'images' folder
            },
          },
        ],
      },
      {
        test: /\.(woff|woff2|eot|ttf|otf)$/,
        use: [
          {
            loader: 'file-loader',
            options:
```

```
            {
                name: '[name].[ext]',
                outputPath: 'fonts/', // Save fonts in the 'fonts' folder
            },
          },
        ],
      },
    ],
  },
};
```

Testing with Webpack

Testing is a crucial part of development. Webpack can be configured to support various testing tools, including Jest and Mocha.

5.1 Configuring and Using Testing Tools

Webpack can be used alongside testing tools like Jest and Mocha to run unit and integration tests.

Installing Jest

Jest is one of the most popular testing frameworks for JavaScript.

```bash
npm install --save-dev jest babel-jest @babel/core @babel/preset-env
```

Webpack Configuration for Jest

Add a basic configuration for Jest:

```javascript
// webpack.config.js
module.exports = {
  // Other configurations...
  module: {
    rules: [
      {
        test: /\.js$/,
        exclude: /node_modules/,
        use: {
          loader: 'babel-loader',
          options: {
            presets: ['@babel/preset-env'],
          },
        },
      },
```

      ],
    },
};
```

##### **Jest Configuration**

Create a `jest.config.js` file to configure Jest:

```javascript
module.exports = {
  preset: 'babel-jest',
  testEnvironment: 'node',
};
```

Example Test with Jest
```

```javascript
// src/index.js
export function add(a, b) {
  return a + b;
}
```

```javascript
// __tests__/index.test.js
import { add } from '../src/index';

test('adds 1 + 2 to equal 3', () => {
  expect(add(1, 2)).toBe(3);
});
```

5.2 Integrating with Mocha

Mocha is a flexible testing framework for JavaScript.

Installing Mocha

```bash
npm install --save-dev mocha chai
```

Mocha Configuration

Create a `test` folder and a test file, for example:

```javascript
// test/index.test.js
const chai = require('chai');
const expect = chai.expect;
```

```javascript
function add(a, b) {
  return a + b;
}

describe('Addition', function() {
  it('should add two numbers', function() {
    expect(add(1, 2)).to.equal(3);
  });
});
```

Running Tests

Add a script in the `package.json` file to run tests with Mocha:

```json
"scripts": {
```

      "test": "mocha"
}
```

### Configuring End-to-End Testing

For end-to-end testing, tools like Cypress and Selenium are useful. Here's an example of configuring Cypress.

#### **6.1 Configuring Cypress**

##### **Installing Cypress**

```bash
npm install --save-dev cypress
```

Adding a Test Script
```

Add a script to run Cypress in the `package.json` file:

```json
"scripts": {
  "cypress": "cypress open"
}
```

Example Test with Cypress

Create a test file in `cypress/integration`:

```javascript
// cypress/integration/sample_spec.js
describe('My First Test', () => {
  it('Visits the Kitchen Sink', () => {
```

```
    cy.visit('https://example.cypress.io')

    cy.contains('type').click()

    cy.url().should('include', '/commands/actions')

    cy.get('.action-email').type('fake@email.com').should('have.value', 'fake@email.com')
  })
})
```

Best Practices

7.1 Project Folder Structure in Webpack

A good folder structure facilitates project management and Webpack configuration. Here is an example structure:

```
project-root/
├── src/
│   ├── components/
│   │   └── App.js
│   ├── assets/
│   │   └── styles.css
│   └── index.js
├── dist/
├── node_modules/
├── .babelrc
├── package.json
├── webpack.config.js
└── tsconfig.json (if using TypeScript)
```

7.2 Versioning and Dependency Management

Managing versions and dependencies is crucial for maintaining a stable project. Use tools like `npm` or `yarn` to manage dependencies and update them regularly. Consider using tools like `npm-check-updates` for automatic updates.

Example of Updating Dependencies

```bash
npx npm-check-updates -u
npm install
```

7.3 Performance and Optimization of Final Bundle

To improve performance and reduce the size of the final bundle, consider the following optimizations:

- **Minimization**: Use plugins like `TerserPlugin` for JavaScript minimization and `OptimizeCSSAssetsPlugin` for CSS.

- **Code Splitting**: Split the code into multiple bundles to load them only when necessary.

- **Caching**: Use file hashing to enable efficient caching.

Example of Bundle Optimization

```javascript
// webpack.config.js
const TerserPlugin = require('terser-webpack-plugin');
const OptimizeCSSAssetsPlugin = require('optimize-css-assets-webpack-plugin');
```

```
module.exports = {
  optimization: {
    minimize: true,
    minimizer: [
      new TerserPlugin(),
      new OptimizeCSSAssetsPlugin(),
    ],
  },
};
```
```

Integrating Webpack with tools like Babel, TypeScript, frameworks, and asset managers is essential for building modern and scalable JavaScript projects. Configuring Webpack for testing and following best practices in dependency management and performance optimization are crucial steps to maintaining an efficient workflow and delivering high-quality products. By implementing these configurations and optimizations, you can
```

ensure that your project is robust, scalable, and ready for production.

Index

1. Introduction to Webpack pg.4

2. Webpack Installation and Configuration pg.35

3. Fundamental Webpack Concepts pg.49

4. Webpack Loaders pg.81

5. Webpack Plugins pg.104

6. Development and Production Modes in Webpack pg.124

7. Integration with Other Tools in Webpack pg.145

www.ingramcontent.com/pod-product-compliance
Lightning Source LLC
Chambersburg PA
CBHW052158220526
45471CB00004B/1715